ELECTION WEEK

Story by Tim Harris

Illustrations by Dana SanMar

Election Week

Text: Tim Harris
Publishers: Tania Mazzeo and Eliza Webb
Series consultant: Amanda Sutera
Hands on Heads Consulting
Editor: Kate Daniel
Project editor: Annabel Smith
Designer: Jess Kelly
Project designer: Danielle Maccarone
Illustrations: Dana SanMar
Production controller: Renee Tome

NovaStar

ISBN 978 0 17 033506 5

Cengage Learning Australia
Level 5, 80 Dorcas Street
Southbank VIC 3006 Australia
Phone: 1300 790 853
Email: aust.nelsonprimary@cengage.com

For learning solutions, visit **cengage.com.au**

Printed in China by 1010 Printing International Ltd
1 2 3 4 5 6 7 29 28 27 26 25

Nelson acknowledges the Traditional Owners and Custodians of the lands of all First Nations Peoples. We pay respect to Elders past and present, and extend that respect to all First Nations Peoples today.

Contents

VOTE FOR ADDIE

Chapter 1

A Crowded Bus

Addie Lane didn't particularly like catching the bus to school. Especially on a Monday morning. There was a hasty energy among the other passengers that seemed to press against her from all sides. To Addie, it signalled the end of the weekend's calm touch.

Not that she didn't like school. Addie loved the quiet rhythm of class and the order that came with learning. She loved seeing her friends and teachers. She loved the opportunities that school provided.

The election.

Addie tried to push the words out of her head. She hadn't yet learnt to manage thoughts that filled her with both hope and terror.

The bus shuddered to a stop, and a new wave of passengers surged onboard. It was bound to be a jam-packed trip.

The young woman on Addie's left who smelled of perfume reached for her phone to check her emails. A schoolboy near the back laughed crudely at a joke. Someone near the front coughed. Then the bus rolled on.

The election.

The words pushed back, and Addie reluctantly agreed to let them settle in her thoughts.

Nominations are due today.

Speeches are on Friday.

As grade five students, Addie's year group had been invited to submit peer nominations for school leadership roles for the following year. Her best friend, Oscar Wang, had vouched to nominate her for a school captain role. This was the hope. But nominees had to present a speech. This was the terror.

There were six positions up for grabs: sports leader, music leader, environmental leader, technology leader and two captain roles – a captain and a vice-captain.

Six positions among a year group of 58 students.

My chances are slim.

Addie was disappointed with herself for being pessimistic. Perhaps it was the stuffiness of the bus that overwhelmed her. Or perhaps it was her fear of public speaking.

The bus jolted to another stop, and Addie watched as more passengers loaded onto the vehicle. It was getting crowded now, and Addie wondered if another bus service had been cancelled and commuters were switching routes.

A teenager glued to his phone made for the back, an elderly man with a fedora hat took up residence behind the driver, and a mother with her baby crammed in next to a schoolboy.

But there was one passenger lagging at the end of the line who caught Addie's attention the most. It was a middle-aged woman with shoulder-length grey hair that bounced with the most perfect curls that Addie had ever seen. The woman was wearing a flowery dress, and the vivid colours on it seemed to light up her face. This lady glowed with life, yet there was a calmness about her that drew Addie in.

The woman swiped her travel card and looked around for a seat. She took a few steps down the aisle, her curls swaying with each step.

She is limping.

Addie noticed that the woman was holding a cane, which she tucked effortlessly under her arm while she steadied herself by holding the back of a seat. The woman's kind eyes searched for an empty spot, but the bus was now full.

The driver checked his mirrors and pushed down on the accelerator. The vehicle lurched to life, and the woman briefly stumbled from her stance. She searched the bus again for a spare seat, and this time her eyes met Addie's.

She's seen me looking. I should offer her my spot.

Addie's father had once badly sprained his ankle on a bushwalking trip. In the weeks after, he had struggled with public transport to and from various medical appointments, often expressing his disappointment at the lack of "common courtesy" among commuters.

"Back in my day, we were taught to stand for passengers who needed a seat more than we did," he had told Addie.

Addie could feel her heart rate rising. She didn't like speaking up in crowded places. She didn't like speaking to strangers. In fact, she didn't like speaking much at all. She suddenly wished her dad had a car and she could be driven to school. But life in the inner suburbs was all about public transport. As much as she didn't like it, it was a part of her routine.

There was another schoolgirl sitting close to the grey-haired woman. Addie wondered why *she* didn't offer *her* spot. Then there was the man with the green jacket, but he was too lost in his book to notice anything else. And the high-school girls near the front were too absorbed in conversation to see beyond their world of gossip.

Addie knew deep down what she had to do. She took a few measured breaths and mustered some courage from within.

Slowly, she waved her hand towards the woman. Then Addie did what she feared most of all – she opened her lips, making way for her quiet voice. "Excuse me, would you like to sit here?"

Chapter 2

Assembly

The school assembly hall was almost as crammed as the bus. But Addie didn't mind the tightness here so much. There was a predictability of Monday's assembly that helped her feel at ease; a sureness that steadied her.

She crossed her legs and sat next to Oscar while the younger grades clumsily arranged themselves at the front of the hall.

Oscar leaned over and whispered in Addie's ear. "You seem happy this morning."

Addie smiled. She was constantly amazed at how well Oscar could read her. She would have to tell him about the bus trip later.

Oscar gently nudged her in the ribs. "I hope that smile means you are *definitely* going for captain. I've been saying for months you'd make a brilliant school captain. I've got my nomination form for you ready to hand in today."

Addie responded by retrieving a small piece of blue paper from her pocket. It was a nomination that she had prepared for Oscar. She knew her friend wanted to make a run for sports leader.

Oscar grinned. "Thanks, Addie. And don't stress about the speeches on Friday. A week is plenty of time to prepare for that."

The school principal, Mrs Uptown, moved to the lectern to signal the start of assembly. After a brief welcome, she took the roving microphone off the stand and walked confidently across to the side of the stage.

"Before we get into teacher announcements, Oscar Wang, who has kindly been organising a lunchtime touch football competition, has a quick message for participants."

Addie's best friend leapt to his feet and bounded onto the stage.

Why is it so easy for him to do this sort of thing?

Addie wasn't jealous. She was proud. She watched in awe as Oscar enthusiastically took the microphone and addressed the assembly.

"Good morning, parents and students ...

I mean parents and teachers ... wait ..."

Everyone laughed. There wasn't a parent in sight.

Oscar briefly lowered the microphone and cracked up at his own mistake. "I mean ... good morning, *teachers* and *students* ... Just a reminder that the touch footy comp finishes on Thursday."

Addie beamed and laughed with the others from her place in the hall. She always admired how nothing seemed to faze Oscar.

Oscar continued his message. "The two leading teams are ..." He paused and scratched his head. "Oh, I wrote this down last night but can't remember now. I think it's the Ducks and the Eagles ... or maybe the Ducks and the Falcons ... Sorry, I"ll get back to you ... Yeah ..."

Mrs Uptown took the microphone. "Thank you, Oscar."

The students applauded loudly as Oscar made his way back to his spot on the floor. There was something likeable about Oscar Wang. While he was prone to making the occasional error, he always got the job done in the end.

Addie gave her friend a big thumbs up.

I wish I had the confidence to speak like that.

The positive energy that Oscar created

quickly vanished with the next announcement. Mrs Uptown lowered her voice – something the children knew all too well represented seriousness.

"Students, I have a very … *disappointing* announcement to make."

The children straightened at this. The principal meant business.

"Somebody has been stealing art supplies from the storeroom in Mr Sandhu's classroom."

Addie exchanged glances with Oscar. News of a thief was bound to cause a stir.

The principal continued. "If anybody knows anything about this, please come and see me in my office. Stealing will not be tolerated."

A lengthy silence hung over the hall like an invisible blanket of guilt. Mrs Uptown was not the sort of principal that the students liked to disappoint. If someone made a big mistake, it was felt throughout the school.

The silence soon made way for intrigue, which rippled across the hall in the form of whispers and turning heads.

Mrs Uptown secured the microphone and clapped her hands to restore the focus. "To finish assembly on a brighter note, this is a reminder for grade five students that all nominations for student leadership positions are due today. Speeches and voting will be on Friday morning. We are very excited about the election, and I'm sure both students and teachers can't wait to exercise the right to vote!"

Oscar took the opportunity to nudge Addie again. "And *I* can't wait to nominate you!"

Chapter 3

Inner Debate

Addie sat on the bus on Tuesday morning with thoughts that rattled around like loose luggage under a passenger seat. It was another crowded trip – her father had confirmed over breakfast that a shortage of drivers had temporarily shut down some routes. But Addie had other things on her mind.

I've been nominated.

Hope had now well and truly danced itself into the week. She had dreamed of running for school captain ever since she first voted in a school election back in grade one.

I have to give a speech on Friday.

The terror was now very real and tangible. This was a problem that had to be dealt with head on. While she had already planned most of her speech, the thought of delivering it on Friday was already pressing in.

There were eight other students who had been nominated for one of the captain roles. Addie was feeling hopeful about her chances, but she was facing tough competition.

Theo Silverman would make a strong contender. He oozed confidence and had a keen following among students in the younger grades. Starring roles in three television commercials in the past year and a scholarship at an acting academy had driven up his popularity.

Then there was Stella Alvarez. Addie couldn't think of a student more competitive and driven than Stella. She was part of the debating club, played flute in the school band, was captain of the school netball team and had been voted into the Student Representative Council four years running. She always had to win.

Rohan Patel was bound to do very well, too. Anyone who achieved a high distinction in a national mathematics competition would draw some votes. He was also full of positivity and had a knack for executing well-timed jokes.

The bus jerked to a stop, and new passengers filed onto the vehicle, filling every vacant seat. Addie placed her bag onto her lap and tucked her elbows in. It was going to be one of those trips.

Why does it have to be so crowded?

The next stop was only a few hundred metres along the road, and Addie dreaded the thought of more people cramming in around her.

The bus soon pulled up to suck in the next wave of passengers. To Addie's surprise, the woman with the perfect grey curls was the first on. She was wearing another flowery dress that seemed to fill the space around her with light. She tapped her travel card, tucked her cane under her arm and walked slowly past the driver. It was obvious she was having some difficulty keeping balance as she stepped over shoes and bags, and Addie knew she had to act fast.

"Would you like this seat?"

Addie's voice was as quiet as ever, but it filled the bus with a gentle kindness that washed over the other passengers.

The woman smiled at Addie in recognition as they swapped places. "You are a thoughtful young lady ... an example to others."

Me? An example to others?

But then something happened that caught Addie off guard.

A teenager made way for an elderly man. "This seat is free."

A schoolgirl put her phone away and stood for the man who was juggling some bags of groceries. "Please, sit here."

A young man with spiky hair stood for a woman who was having trouble finding something to hold for balance.

The ripple effect. Dad taught me about this. Sometimes things spread – both good and bad.

Addie couldn't believe what she was seeing. Strangers were smiling and interacting with each other. The invisible walls between passengers seemed to have tumbled down.

Now standing, gripping a pole, Addie let her thoughts return to the election. How would she find the courage to give her speech on Friday? Speaking on a noisy bus was one thing, but addressing an entire hall of watching eyes and listening ears was another thing altogether. She swallowed hard.

When the bus finally pulled into Addie's stop, she was almost beside herself with fear.

"Are you okay?" The woman with the grey curls gently stopped Addie as they got off the bus.

Addie nodded. "Yes."

Why can't I just admit that I'm nervous about my speech?

The woman stooped to Addie's level. Her eyes fizzed with kindness. "Well, I'm glad you're okay. You are a compassionate soul, I can tell. What happened on the bus this morning was simply terrific. The positive act of a young schoolgirl – *you* – sent ripples through those passengers."

She knows about the ripple effect too.

Addie soaked the words in. The grey-haired woman spoke with warmth and authority, and it was difficult not to be pulled into the message.

The woman straightened and balanced on her cane. "Well, you have a wonderful day. I'd best be off."

Addie spotted something in the woman's shoulder bag as she turned to leave. It was a primary school maths textbook. And for a moment, she forgot all about her speech and the election and suddenly remembered something that had slipped her mind.

I promised I would meet Mischa in the library to help her study for her maths test.

Addie walked along Wood Street thinking of a plan of attack to help Mischa. The grade three student was relying on her help to master multiplication.

It was a much quieter path to school this way.

It was less crowded than Kelso Road – just the way she liked it.

As she reached school and made her way to the library to meet Mischa, Oscar bounded up to her from the playground.

"Addie, you won't believe it! The thief has struck again! Let's meet at lunch to work out a way to catch them!"

Chapter 4

Plan of Attack

Addie and Oscar sat in the shade of their favourite gum tree. Splotches of midday sunlight slipped through the leaves overhead, warming their skin with the promise of summer. Tuesday lunch was their regular hang-out slot as it was the only time they were both free.

"The thief is already giving us clues," explained Oscar. "Mr Sandhu's storeroom is the target, and the thief has struck before school on both occasions – I heard Mrs Uptown and Mr Sandhu talking about it."

Addie listened closely and scribbled some notes in her purple writing book. "Do you *really* think we can catch the thief?"

Oscar almost choked on his sandwich with laughter. "Do I *really* think we can catch a thief?

Of course! We are the dream team of reliability, Addie. You and I get stuff done."

"I suppose so."

"Who was it that helped Ms Walters organise the Book Week parade?" Oscar was determined to make a point.

"Us," said Addie.

"Who was it that sorted out the grade two buddy system?"

"Us."

"And who will catch the thief?"

Addie allowed herself to smile. "Us."

Oscar scanned the playground to make sure nobody was within earshot. "We need to arrive at school super early tomorrow and stake out Mr Sandhu's classroom."

"Like one of those police stake-outs on TV?" Addie was warming to the idea. She envisioned herself wearing a black leather jacket and chowing down on a doughnut while she waited to leap on an unsuspecting burglar.

"Exactly," said Oscar, as though he was reading Addie's mind. "We can hide in the bushes between the library and the grade four rooms."

Addie jotted more notes into her book. She was so excited about the stake-out idea that she didn't notice Hunter Pedroni amble up to where she and Oscar were sitting. The grade one student had tear-streaked cheeks, and she was sniffling miserably.

"I can't tie my shoelaces."

Addie looked up from her notes. "Hi, Hunter. I didn't see you there. It's okay, I can teach you how to do it."

Addie got to work right away. She explained quietly to Hunter how the laces worked together and how to tie a knot. She patiently watched as Hunter attempted to do the same, then comforted the young student as she burst out crying because the knot slipped loose.

"Let's try again. You can do it."

Oscar watched on as Addie weaved her magic, demonstrating the steps before Hunter tried again.

"That's the way, Hunter," said Addie. "Keep your fingers pressed there and then bring the other lace through."

Hunter glowed as she sat back and examined the knot. "I did it! Thank you."

And with that, Hunter was off and racing about with her friends.

"You're good like that," said Oscar.

I like helping people.

Oscar pointed to the other side of the playground where Stella Alvarez was marching around, handing out what were no doubt election flyers and plastering posters to the sides of buildings. "Hmm. It looks like Stella is on the campaign trail."

"Stella would make a good captain," said Addie with a sigh. "Her speech will be one of the best. I don't think I can compete against her."

I don't want to give a speech on Friday.

Oscar read Addie's face like a book. "Promise me that you will work on your speech tonight. Promise me that you will go through with this. After what you told me happened on the bus yesterday morning–"

"And today!" Addie beamed. "The same lady got on the bus this morning. She mentioned the ripple effect."

"Look at you – chatting to other passengers on the bus. You're changing, Addie. You're growing in confidence." Oscar smiled before taking a bite out of his sandwich.

The pair were interrupted when their class teacher, Ms Walters, approached. "I thought I would find you two here." The teacher handed a piece of paper to Oscar. "These are the team lists for the last round of touch football on Thursday."

"Thanks, Ms Walters."

The teacher leaned against the tree and looked out over the buzzing playground. "I'm really going to miss this place when I leave for my stint in the country."

"We will all miss you too," said Addie. "It's a shame you won't be here for the student elections on Friday."

Ms Walters looked down at Addie with a soft gaze. "Promise me one thing, Addie Lane. You give that speech everything you've got."

I'm not sure I can.

Chapter 5

The Stake-Out

Addie left home with plenty of time to meet Oscar for the stake-out. She had never caught the "early early" bus before. This trip – two whole timetable slots before her regular journey – was quieter than she could have imagined. There were entirely empty seats, and Addie was able to put her schoolbag between herself and the aisle.

I like it like this.

As was becoming routine, Addie's stomach twisted when she thought about her speech on Friday. She had spent the previous night typing it on the computer and printing it onto palm cards, but when she tried to practise in front of her father, she could barely even hear her own voice.

I can always withdraw my nomination. I don't have to go through with this.

Doubt flooded Addie's thoughts like a burst dam swamping a town. But it was much easier to let the doubt in than to sandbag her mind with courage. Courage took effort, and fear had swallowed courage whole.

When she arrived at school, she met Oscar in the bushes next to the library. Her friend, as always, was early and had been waiting for fifteen minutes.

"No movement yet," said Oscar. "Mr Sandhu hasn't arrived, so his classroom is still locked."

Addie nodded. "Mr Sandhu has playground duty on Wednesday. He should be here soon."

As if on cue, the grade four teacher appeared from around the corner of the staffroom block and made a beeline for his classroom. Addie and Oscar, slightly panicked, pushed themselves deeper into the bush to hide. The last thing they wanted was for Mr Sandhu to suspect either of them as the thief.

"That was a little too close for comfort," whispered Oscar. "He nearly saw us."

Addie held her finger to her lips.

Mr Sandhu soon reappeared wearing a pink fluorescent jacket and a broad-brimmed hat.

Oscar leaned towards Addie.

"Huh. The jacket suits him," he said.

Addie stifled a laugh as she thought back to a funny assembly skit that Theo Silverman did wearing the same pink jacket. He had the whole school in stitches as he mimicked Mr Sandhu on stage.

Addie was glad for this distraction. Catching a thief allowed her to think about something else other than her speech.

There was not much action for the first ten minutes of the stake-out. Apart from the occasional teacher who walked in and out of the staffroom, the pair of detectives didn't spot anything of note.

That was until Dylan Sommers – a small blond-haired boy in grade one – marched up the steps of Mr Sandhu's classroom.

Addie clutched Oscar. Could this be the thief? She could hear Dylan rummaging around inside Mr Sandhu's room. What was he up to?

Clank!

A loud metallic rattle suddenly came from inside the room. It sounded like Dylan had knocked over a tin of pencils.

"What's he doing in there?" whispered Oscar.

Dylan soon emerged from the room carrying

a bulging cotton bag. He looked around as if finding his bearings – at one point gazing directly into the bush where Addie and Oscar were frozen in place. Addie was certain they would be spotted. After a tense few seconds, Dylan walked along a path in the direction of his classroom.

Would a grade one student be bold enough to steal – and in broad daylight?

Addie wasn't sure. But she didn't have time to dwell on it because another student had appeared on the steps to Mr Sandhu's room.

It was Kayla Lee – the current grade six environmental leader. Unlike Dylan, Kayla was swift and efficient in whatever she was doing. She ducked into the room and exited only a minute or so later carrying a large cardboard box.

What's inside the box?

How Addie wished to know. She could sense Oscar was just as eager to find out too.

"Should we follow her?" Addie suggested.

"No. We have two suspects now," said Oscar. "Let's wait until the bell rings in case anyone else pops into the room."

But nobody else did. The rest of the stake-out was uneventful. When the bell eventually rang, announcing the beginning of class, Addie and

Oscar zipped quickly to their room and pulled out their pencil cases.

Ms Walters was just about to write something on the board when the loudspeakers at the front of the room erupted to life. It was Mrs Uptown.

"Attention, all students and staff. It appears there has been another theft of art supplies from Mr Sandhu's storeroom. Anyone with information is urged to come forward."

Addie exchanged glances with Oscar.

It can only be one of two people: Dylan Sommers or Kayla Lee.

But then Oscar did something unexpected. He made a signal towards Addie to keep her lips closed. What was her friend up to?

Chapter 6

Group Work

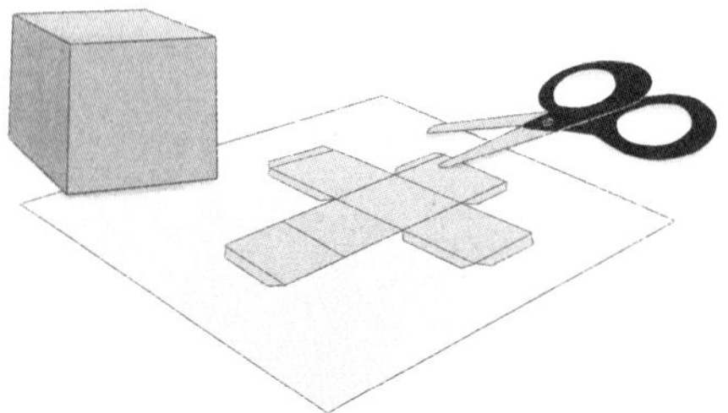

The first lesson of the day was mathematics. Ms Walters split the students into groups of four and asked them to create nets of three-dimensional shapes.

"I'll give you forty-five minutes," explained the teacher. "After that, each group will be asked to present their work. Be sure to look for patterns. What connections can you make about the number of faces, edges and corners in each shape? How many nets can you create?"

Addie was grouped with Oscar, Stella and Aiden. She was glad to have Oscar by her side. Having her best friend next to her was like having a blanket in a storm. It put her at ease in social situations that would otherwise press in against her.

As the students made their way to their workstations, Oscar pulled Addie aside. “Let’s keep the information we know about Dylan and Kayla to ourselves for another day. I have a plan.”

Addie wasn’t so sure. “But Mrs Uptown said that anyone with information should come forward.”

Oscar shook his head. “Trust me. Give it one more day before we share anything. I’ll fill you in later.”

“We don’t want to get into trouble for not saying anything.”

“We won’t ... I’m sure of it.”

Addie knew enough about Oscar to know that he had good intentions. He didn’t like getting into trouble and would never put her at risk. Whatever he had planned, she would hear about it later.

The students quickly set to work, examining a range of plastic shapes and sketching out quick drafts of nets. Meanwhile, Stella took it upon herself to hand out the stationery, and she kept a close eye on progress.

“Don’t waste time,” she snapped at Oscar when he and Aiden joked about shape names.

Once the group was satisfied with the rough drawings, they used rulers and lead pencils to neatly arrange the nets on coloured cardboard.

Stella was finding her stride, and she continued bossing the group around like she was in charge. "Make sure you cut neatly."

"You got it," said Oscar.

"I think Addie should be our group presenter," said Stella in a matter-of-fact voice. "She never says anything in class."

Addie's heart froze. It wasn't up to Stella to decide who spoke, was it? "It's okay ... someone else can talk," she managed in defence.

"I'm happy to do it," replied Oscar quickly, stepping between his friend and trouble.

Stella stood firm. "No, as the leader of this group, I nominate Addie."

Please don't make me do this.

"It's decided then," snapped Stella. "You are our spokesperson. I'm not going to do it, and Oscar already spoke at assembly on Monday. It's *your* turn." A smirk flickered on Stella's face as she cornered Addie. "And anyway," she added, "it will be good practice for Friday's speech."

Oscar put his scissors down firmly. "What about you, Aiden? Would you like to present?"

"Not really," replied Aiden, clearly unaware that Stella was ambushing Addie.

Ms Walters walked past the group.

“How is this group going?” she asked.

“Addie has volunteered to be our group presenter,” lied Stella. There was a hidden nastiness – one that was designed only for Addie to hear – in her voice.

Addie could feel herself turning pale. Stella’s competitive streak had gone to a whole new level.

“Well done, Addie,” said Ms Walters.

When Ms Walters clapped her hands a few minutes later, Addie could barely breathe. The pressing feeling was making it difficult to focus.

“To the floor, thank you, students,” said the teacher.

The pressing feeling was hurting Addie’s chest. It was like she was being squeezed between the hands of a giant. And to make matters worse, Ms Walters invited Addie’s group to share first.

Stella hastily prodded the rest of the group into position and turned to face her classmates. “Addie is our speaker,” she said briskly, giving Addie no chance to back down.

Ms Walters offered Addie a smile that showed she believed in her. “We look forward to hearing what your group found out about nets.”

Addie could feel all her classmates’ eyes on her; it was adding to the tightness in her chest.

Her mouth was dry. She took a deep breath.

"I ... er ... *we* made some ..."

"Go on," encouraged the teacher, with another smile. "Take your time and think about what you learnt."

Addie was stuck. She was so rattled that it had shaken all clarity out of her thoughts. The only thing she could think of was *not* wanting to speak in front of everyone.

"Tell them," said Stella, with the same hidden nastiness she had used before.

Addie shuffled slightly on the carpet. She could feel her shoes scuffing up the blue carpet. "We ... we made some shapes ... nets ..."

An awkward pause followed. It was so long that Ms Walters had no choice but to palm the speaking off to Stella. "Perhaps you can fill us in."

As Stella launched into a deviously well-delivered speech about three-dimensional shapes and their nets, Addie mustered the strength to give clarity to a single thought.

I'm pulling out of the election. I can't do this.

Chapter 7

The Suspects

Addie got to school early again on Thursday and met Oscar in the bushes near Mr Sandhu's classroom.

Oscar had shared his plan with Addie the day before. However, she had found it difficult to concentrate on what he was saying because her maths talk had gone so badly.

"Are you sure you're okay?" Oscar had asked as he told her the plan.

Addie had nodded, but her thoughts were elsewhere.

Today, she was still distracted. As she crawled in next to Oscar, she badly wanted to tell him that she was going to pull out of the election. The school needed confident leaders, she had decided, not shy students who couldn't string a sentence together in front of their peers.

With her mind made up about her election withdrawal, Addie trained her attention on the plan. Oscar had convinced her that they needed more evidence before they shared anything with Mrs Uptown. “It’s not fair to accuse Dylan and Kayla when we don’t know what they were carrying. Innocent until proven guilty, right?”

They waited patiently – hidden in the dark leaves of the shrubby bush – until Dylan meandered towards Mr Sandhu’s room.

“What did I tell you yesterday?” whispered Oscar. “He might come back for one of two reasons: he is the thief, or he is doing a job for his teacher.”

Addie watched on as Dylan made his way up the steps and into Mr Sandhu’s classroom. Like the day before, she could hear him rummaging around somewhere inside. A clanking sound was followed by a rattle.

“Just like yesterday,” said Addie.

Dylan soon made his exit. He was carrying a bulky bag, and it looked to be heavy.

“Could be art supplies,” hissed Oscar excitedly. “I’ll follow Dylan ... You stay and wait to see if anyone else comes along – especially Kayla.”

Oscar slipped stealthily from the bushes and followed Dylan as he made his way towards the grade one rooms. Addie watched as her friend ducked behind the corner of the building, glancing this way and that as he kept a safe distance between himself and suspect number one.

Suspect number two was Addie's responsibility. She stilled herself completely in the bushes and kept an eye out.

Who needs to be a captain when you can be a spy?

Addie shook her head. It wasn't like her to be so negative. Perhaps she was putting herself under too much pressure. Perhaps she needed to relax about the election. Perhaps she shouldn't withdraw her nomination. She'd dreamed of being a captain for years.

Don't let yourself be fooled by hope. It's easier to let terror win.

Kayla's appearance almost startled Addie because she'd been so lost in her thoughts. She watched as the environmental leader moved swiftly up the steps and into the grade four classroom.

"What is she up to?" Addie whispered to herself.

Kayla returned to the top of the steps shortly

after, carrying another large cardboard box.

Kayla could be the thief.

Taking inspiration from Oscar's stealthy detective work, Addie eased her way out of the bushes and tiptoed to the nearest corner of a building, being sure not to be seen by Kayla. Her heart was thumping loudly, perhaps on par with the wild hammering she felt in the maths lesson the day before.

Addie continued following Kayla towards the grade six rooms. At one point, Kayla turned around to say hello to some of her classmates who were sitting on the silver seats near the walkway. Addie had to dive into the girls' bathroom to avoid detection.

That was close.

Kayla eventually made her way to her classroom and carried the box inside, unaware she was being closely tailed.

Curiosity was now eating away at Addie; she *had* to know what was in the box. Oscar's words kept ringing in her ears. "Innocent until proven guilty, right?"

She crouched beneath the window of Kayla's classroom, daring herself to rise up and peek inside.

What if she sees me? I don't want to be caught spying.

No, *I have to do this for the sake of the school. Mrs Uptown said that stealing will not be tolerated.*

With that, Addie stood up and pressed her face against the glass. And right as she did, Kayla Lee, who had opened the box and was emptying out its contents, looked right back at her.

Chapter 8

Kayla Lee

"Have you been following me, Addie?" called Kayla from inside the classroom.

Addie could only nod. She had grown up knowing that the truth was always the best option. Her father had drilled it into her from a young age. Besides, she'd been busted.

Kayla signalled for Addie to join her inside the room. She wasn't frowning. She wasn't suspicious. She was simply smiling.

"Why did you follow me?" asked Kayla. "Did you think I was the art thief?" She pointed to the box and threw Addie a questioning look.

The contents of the box came as a big surprise to Addie. It was maths equipment. A collection of electronic scales and wooden balancing arms were laid out on the desk. She remembered using them in grade four.

Kayla ran her finger over one of the balancing scales. “Mr Sandhu has ordered some more resources, but until they arrive, we have to share the measurement equipment with his class.”

“Oh, I see. Oscar and I thought you might have been the thief,” admitted Addie.

Kayla laughed. “Me? No, I’m just fetching something for my teacher. But good on you for trying to find out who it might be.”

As if a light switch had been flicked on, the expression on Kayla’s face changed. Her smile vanished, and she pressed her lips together. For a moment, Addie thought she might be in trouble.

“I’ve been busy with environmental projects this week,” said Kayla. “But I’ve been meaning to find out who’s in the running for the leadership positions next year. Who is going for the captain roles?”

Addie felt a tiny press on her chest. “Oh … Theo Silverman and Rohan Patel are in the running … and Stella Alvarez … and some others.”

“What about you, Addie?” Kayla’s voice was sincere.

Be honest.

“No … I don’t think I will,” said Addie. “I mean, I got nominated … but I am going to pull out this morning … I need to talk to Ms Walters about it.”

Kayla's mouth popped open. "What? You got nominated and you are going to pull out? You can't do that. You would be *silly* not to go for it!"

The tiny flicker of hope inside Addie's heart burned brighter at these words. "You really think I should run?"

"Give me one good reason why you should pull out," said Kayla.

Terror.

Addie paused and looked down at her shoes. Apart from her father and Oscar, she had never opened up to anybody about her deep fear of public speaking. Yet here she was, possibly seconds away from spilling her secrets with a grade six student.

But somehow it felt right. She had grown tired of trying to wrestle her thoughts to the ground and bury them with a truckload of self-doubt. Wouldn't it be easier to release the pressure and talk to somebody about it?

Kayla's genuine tone put Addie more at ease. "It's okay ... you can talk to me. I went through the same thing last year. I almost pulled out of the election myself because I get nervous when I have to give speeches."

At this, Addie looked up from her shoes.

"You're scared of making speeches? That's what I'm scared of, too," she admitted. "Speeches fill me with ..." Her eyes rolled towards the ceiling as she searched for the right word. "Terror."

Addie exhaled. She had let it out. She had finally – audibly – revealed her fear to somebody who might be able to help.

Kayla must have spotted the relief on Addie's face. "Addie, leaders don't only lead with their words. They can lead with their actions. I've seen you helping around the school." She chuckled for a moment. "I've even seen you try to catch a thief!"

Addie smiled.

"You *have* to run in this election," continued Kayla. "Don't let fear stop you. Just read your speech off a piece of paper – that's what I did. I know I'm not skilled at public speaking, but I have a passion for the environment, and I'm good at organising things. Elections are great like that ... they give lots of people a chance to show their skills and passions. You, Addie ... you create ripples of kindness."

Ripples.

The morning bell sounded, and Addie headed to class with a spring in her step. She retrieved a farewell card from her bag and put it on Ms Walters' desk on her way past.

Something glowed and pulsated through Addie's body that Thursday morning. She didn't even mind that much when Oscar explained that the thief was still at large – Dylan Sommers, like Kayla Lee, was only doing a job for his teacher.

But nothing could sidetrack Addie. Hope was surging through her entire being.

I can do this.

Chapter 9

The Speech

The whole school gathered on the floor of the hall first thing on Friday. Election day had brought with it a warm breeze that drifted through the open doors – a reminder that summer was just around the corner. Excited chatter flitted between the students as they waited for Mrs Uptown to take the microphone.

I can do this.

Addie had been repeating these words in her head since her chat with Kayla. She had rehearsed her speech several times the night before and was not going to let the opportunity slip.

"Good morning, students," Mrs Uptown said from the stage. "This election is a privilege for everyone. It is a reminder that we *each* have a say in who leads us. All students and teachers will vote."

The principal continued, "We've even had an early vote from Ms Walters whose last day was yesterday. Did you know that early voting is allowed in real government elections?"

The students gasped at this. But they were also eager to hear from the candidates. Some of the grade one students were already squirming.

Mrs Uptown turned around to face the candidates. "A reminder that speeches must be kept to one minute."

The principal then set to work introducing the candidates for each position in groups. The first to give speeches were those running for sports leader.

Addie clapped loudly when Oscar made his speech. It was littered with his usual jumble of words, but it was also saturated with his trademark passion and enthusiasm.

Voting for sports leader occurred immediately after the speeches. A team of teachers collected the voting slips from each class and got counting right away. All results would be announced at the end of assembly.

The speeches and voting for music leader, environmental leader and technology leader passed by quickly.

As the line of candidates shrunk, Addie, who was sitting at the end of the line and would be last to give her speech, could feel the pressing teasing her chest. But there was no backing out now.

I can do this.

Theo Silverman was up first. He dazzled the entire assembly hall with a speech filled with charisma, desire and wit. He was a natural; a performer; a confident leader.

How can I compete against this?

Self-doubt made the pressing squeeze tighter. The unwelcome burden of negative feelings that had plagued Addie all week was threatening to return. It crawled over her skin and prickled her face. It crept into her thoughts and tried to hijack the hope that Kayla had given her.

Don't let terror win. You can do this.

The line continued to shrink until there were only two candidates left. Stella Alvarez would give the penultimate speech.

As Addie had expected, Stella's presentation was as immaculate as her polished shoes. But Addie remembered how mean Stella had been to her in the maths lesson.

Is that how leaders should behave?

Addie was surprised when Mrs Uptown called

Stella aside after her speech. The principal guided Stella behind the curtains and out of view of the audience. Only an uncomfortable Addie could see what was going on.

Mr Sandhu appeared from the wings and joined the principal behind the curtain. He was holding a box of paint and glitter and glue, which he placed on the floor in front of Stella.

What's going on?

Stella's face dropped at the sight of the box. Addie could just make out the sound of Mrs Uptown's voice. "Stealing will not be tolerated. I'll talk to you after voting."

Stella is the art thief!

It made perfect sense to Addie now. Stella's competitive streak had brought out the worst in her. She had hung brightly decorated posters all over the school. She often came in early before band practice and it looked like she'd been stealing supplies.

Mrs Uptown walked briskly to the microphone to address the school. "Apologies for the delay ... We just had to sort out a ... *technical* issue. And now, without further ado, I would like to invite Addie Lane to give her speech."

Addie was thrown. What she had just

witnessed had completely put her off.

I don't think I can do this.

A strange numbness took control of her body. She couldn't feel anything but panic as she walked quietly to the microphone and unfolded her speech. Terror had risen again and was pressing from all sides.

An uncomfortable silence filled the hall. Addie was frozen. It was just like the maths lesson. She didn't have the nerve to look out at her peers – and certainly not her teachers.

"You've got this."

A quiet whisper sounded from somewhere near the front of the hall. On reflex, Addie looked up to see who had spoken.

The current grade six leaders sat on chairs near the edge of the stage. Addie scanned their faces to see where the encouraging voice had come from, and it only took her a moment to find the owner. It was Kayla. Her new friend was smiling proudly at her and gave a thumbs up.

Addie looked around a little more. She quickly spotted Mischa, who she had been helping with maths. The young girl beamed at her.

Then her eyes found Hunter Pedroni in the front row. Hunter's shoelaces were tied neatly, and she responded to the eye contact with something that got her into trouble from her teacher: “Go, Addie!” she called.

Lastly, she found Oscar. He nodded towards her, reminding her of the encouragement he had been giving for weeks.

Addie lifted the piece of paper in her hands and held it steadily. She scanned the first couple of lines and rehearsed them in her mind. As she breathed slowly and prepared to read, she allowed a sweet feeling to fill her entire being.

Hope.

Chapter 10

The Results

I did it.

Addie was incredibly proud of herself for getting through the speech. It wasn't the most entertaining presentation of the day, but that didn't matter to her. The words she had penned – read quietly and steadily from the microphone at the front of the hall – were sincere and heartfelt. She managed to say everything she had dreamed of since voting in that first election back in grade one.

Thanks to the efficiency of the counting by the teachers, the students were able to enter the hall for the results after a quick ten-minute stretch outside.

The microphone squealed to life, and Mrs Uptown shooshed the audience by displaying the school crest on the big screen. “It is always exciting to be able to announce our leaders for next year.”

The students leaned forward, eager to hear who the new leaders would be.

Addie was thrilled for Oscar when his name was read out as the incoming sports leader. He was an obvious choice, and Addie was sure he would have won in a landslide.

The music, environmental and technology leaders were announced shortly after, and each of the newly elected students joined Oscar on the stage.

“And finally, it is my pleasure to announce the two incoming captains,” said Mrs Uptown as Mr Sandhu handed her a piece of paper with the latest count.

Deep breaths. Remember, be happy for whoever is voted in.

Addie’s hands were pressed tightly into her lap. She couldn’t even bring herself to blink in case she missed anything.

Mrs Uptown’s gaze lingered on the slip of paper for a moment. “This is very unusual,” she said. “We have a clear leader for captain, and a tie for vice-captain.”

The students gasped loudly. This was a first.

Mr Sandhu whispered something in Mrs Uptown's ear.

"Yes … good idea," said the principal, still close enough to the microphone that her voice echoed across the hall. "We would usually announce the vice-captain first, but we might flip that around while the teachers double-check the voting in that race." She paused. "I am pleased to announce that Theo Silverman is the incoming captain!"

Everyone cheered as Theo bounded to the stage and joined the other incoming leaders. They welcomed him with big smiles and clapping.

He is a good choice.

Addie was pleased for her classmate. Deep down, she knew he was cut out for the role. Captains were expected to give most of the speeches, while vice-captains played an important helping role – one that Addie knew she would be good at if given the chance.

Mrs Uptown waited patiently as Mr Sandhu ducked off the stage to check the counting. Addie watched the principal closely, hoping for a sign – a signal – that she might be elected.

And then it happened.

Mrs Uptown, who was as professional as

principals come, briefly let her guard slip. Her eyes flashed between Addie and the boy next to her on the assembly floor – Rohan Patel.

It's between me and Rohan.

Addie was sure of it. And she was sure that nobody else would have picked up on that fleeting glance. It was a gut feeling – something deep down inside of her sparked by the look in the principal's eye – that made her so certain.

Mr Sandhu soon returned to the stage and showed Mrs Uptown a new piece of paper.

She leaned towards the microphone. "How unusual … votes have been rechecked and I can confirm that we have a dead heat …"

But just when Addie thought things couldn't get more interesting, a loud voice called from the back of the hall, causing several of the students to spin around in bewilderment.

"Is it too late to cast a vote?"

Addie recognised the voice, but she couldn't place it. She spun around and saw someone familiar. It was the grey-haired lady from the bus.

I don't believe it.

"Mrs Robson," said Mrs Uptown from the stage, "of course, as the newest member of our school, you are welcome to vote. Students,

Mrs Robson is the replacement teacher for Ms Walters until the end of the year."

The students clapped politely as the new teacher made her way to the front.

Mrs Robson's dress filled the hall with colour. Her curls swayed gracefully as she limped up the steps of the stage. Confidence was something that this teacher didn't lack.

"May I take the microphone?" she asked, expertly unclipping it from the stand before Mrs Uptown could reply.

I still don't believe it.

Addie felt like she was the only student in the hall who knew where things were going. Hope was transforming itself into destiny.

"You may be wondering why I should vote if I don't know all the students," said Mrs Robson. "But I met a real leader on the bus this week – I don't drive, you see, because of my bad hip. But I'll bore my grade five class with that rock climbing story later."

The students giggled.

"I met a student from this school who showed that leaders don't always have to use words. No, leaders come in all shapes and sizes, and many choose to lead by their actions. They create ripples of kindness."

With that, Mrs Robson lowered the microphone and said something to Mrs Uptown, before pointing directly to Addie, who didn't mind when every student turned to face her. The pressing feeling had disappeared.

Mrs Uptown scrunched up the piece of paper. "Well, that vote breaks the tie. Addie Lane is your incoming vice-captain. Well done, Addie!"

Addie leapt to her feet and skipped to the stage so lightly that she could barely feel the soles of her feet.

"You'll make a great vice-captain," said Theo, patting her on the back. "And I can help you with your speeches whenever you need."

"Thanks, Theo. Congratulations to you!"

Addie hugged Oscar and turned to face the school. She would never forget election week.